ANGEL MEDITATION

GUIDED MEDITATION TO LEARN TO CONNECT, COMMUNICATE, AND HEAL WITH YOUR ARCHANGEL AND GUARDIAN ANGEL

ADESH SILVA

CONTENTS

Introduction   5

1. The Foundations of the Higher Powers   11
2. Archangels and Guided Meditation   28
3. Angels and Guided Meditation   44
4. Guardian Angels and Guided Meditation   61
5. Looking Into Your Future   71

Conclusion   85
References   91

© **Copyright 2020 - All rights reserved.**

The content contained within this book may not be reproduced, duplicated or transmitted without direct written permission from the author or the publisher.

Under no circumstances will any blame or legal responsibility be held against the publisher, or author, for any damages, reparation, or monetary loss due to the information contained within this book, either directly or indirectly.

Legal Notice:

This book is copyright protected. It is only for personal use. You cannot amend, distribute, sell, use, quote or paraphrase any part, or the content within this book, without the consent of the author or publisher.

Disclaimer Notice:

Please note the information contained within this document is for educational and entertainment purposes only. All effort has been executed to present accurate, up to date, reliable, complete information. No warranties of any kind are declared or implied. Readers acknowledge that the author is not engaged in the rendering of legal, financial, medical or professional advice. The content within this book has been derived from various sources. Please consult a licensed professional before attempting any techniques outlined in this book.

By reading this document, the reader agrees that under no circumstances is the author responsible for any losses, direct or indirect, that are incurred as a result of the use of the information contained within this document, including, but not limited to, errors, omissions, or inaccuracies.

INTRODUCTION

What is the first question you would ask your guardian angel? Take a moment to sit back and think about the direction your life is heading and note any question that pops into your mind. For example, do you want to know whether or not you should go back to school? Maybe you're at the crossroads in your relationship and you want advice on which way to go. Between the archangels, angels, and your guardian angels, you can have any question answered once you learn how to communicate with these higher powers.

Some people refer to angels, archangels, and guardian angels as *higher powers*, which is the term I'll use when talking about all of them in this book. You also hear people refer to them simply as *angels*.

Then there are many people who refer to each archangel and even their guardian angels by name. There are so many different ways to refer to the higher powers because they're a part of a realm where you follow what you believe. For example, most people know there are archangels, which are the most powerful angels in the higher realm, and then there are angels. They know that the archangels work closely with the angels, who take care of the world. This is known as the hierarchy of angels. Some people believe that each archangel has certain angels that they manage in the otherworld, while other people believe that they all work together.

One of the most important points I want you to understand right away is that this book isn't meant to make you believe anything you don't want to. For instance, I believe that archangels, angels, and guardian angels are all in the "spirit guides" category, while other people will refer to spirit guides as only our guardian angels because they work closely with us every day. It's up to you to believe what you want, but for the purposes of this book, I'll keep archangels, angels, and guardian angels as separate entities. I do believe in spirit guides, but they're a different type of entity, which you'll learn about in chapter 5.

I also want to point out that I believe there are differences between the archangels, angels, and guardian angels. I will discuss their differences and even similarities in the following chapters. I'll also explain how you can communicate with each of these higher powers and how they communicate with you.

The history of these higher powers is one that you can't really pin down. Some people look to the Bible to track their history. Other people simply focus on the fact that God created the angels to help him stay connected with people, animals, and all living things in the world. There are also those who believe that they've always just been a part of the universe and they're not the creation of any higher power.

Commonly, you'll read that archangels were created before angels. They battled evil entities to win the world, and they helped preserve it so that humans, animals, and others could inhabit it. Once the earth became filled with plant life, people, and animals, the angels helped in managing it to ensure that everyone received the help they needed. Angels also guide people and spread to them the messages of the higher powers. Generally, angels were created from the same energy as archangels;

however, they don't hold the same amount of power.

You'll start your journey learning about angel meditation by understanding the foundations of the higher powers. You'll learn the benefits that communicating with them will give you and also become aware of any blocks that can weaken your connection. You'll also receive some of my best tips for communication. Then we'll dive into the similarities and differences between the higher powers so you know whom to talk to and when.

I will start helping you communicate with the archangels first because they oversee the angels and guardian angels. They're at the top of the angel hierarchy. Not only will you learn how to communicate with them through guided meditation, but you'll also learn about the seven main archangels and their special roles.

Under the archangels are the angels. They often carry messages from your guardians to the archangels so you can achieve your life's purpose. They also help you connect with other people, whether they're your loved ones who already moved on to heaven or someone miles away. You'll learn about the main types of angels, their roles, and how to communicate with them.

As you continue on your journey, you'll discover your guardian angels. They are the ones who work the closest to you. If you pay close enough attention, you'll see messages from them on a daily basis. While they can easily communicate with you, it's still important to reach out to them for clarity or any type of help that you need. It's their job to not only protect you but also guide you throughout the course of your life. They choose to be with you so they're dedicated to your emotional, psychological, physical, and spiritual well-being.

Finally, this part of your journey will end by looking toward your future. No matter what you believe when it comes to the higher powers, it's up to you to strengthen the communication. It's up to you to take the time to notice the signs and maybe complete a little research so you can get a clear message. You need to make time to take care of your mindset and remain calm, even in moments of chaos.

Before you launch into learning about angel meditation, it's time to take a step back and focus on you. Clear your mind and open up your heart to what you're about to digest. Allow the words to flow to you like a calm river so you can start to open up your spiritual doorway immediately. This isn't a book that you need to rush through. It's important to take your time so you can build your beliefs and line of communication as you go.

THE FOUNDATIONS OF THE HIGHER POWERS

You'll build the best foundation to communicate with the higher powers when you have an open mind. You don't need to believe everything that you read, but you should believe everything that you feel. Your intuition or gut is the strongest indicator that the higher powers are trying to give you a message. What you feel from this message and what your intuition tells you to believe is what you need to follow. If you try to visit with your spirit guides or get answers from your questions but don't fully believe what you feel or hear, you won't receive the whole message.

Communicating with your higher powers means that you're open to their powers. You give them 100 percent trust that they'll help guide you down the right path. You also put trust in yourself to follow the messages that you receive from them. For example, if you look at the clock every day at 11:11, your guardian angels are trying to tell you that a gateway has opened up for you and your thoughts are beginning to manifest into a reality. What does this mean for you? It means that you need to be mindful of your thoughts and focus on your goals. If you want to do well in school, you have to stay dedicated to your schoolwork and study for tests. Your spirit guides will see to it that you're rewarded with good grades.

Benefits of Higher Power Communication

Your soul started working with your spirit guides even before you were born. You met with them to understand the path that you need to follow so you can learn certain life lessons. However, once your soul enters the body, you don't remember these lessons so the spiritual entities work to help you by giving you signs through numbers, which are often referred to as angel numbers. They are also in your dreams and intuition, and they even talk to you directly if your connection is strong enough. Through this connection, you'll feel many benefits that'll help you continue to strengthen your bond with your spirit guides.

1. ***Your intuition will continue to increase.*** This is the gut feeling that you have that helps you make decisions. For example, you meet someone and they ask you out on a date, but your "gut" is telling you to say no, so you follow its advice. You don't know why your intuition told you it was a bad idea, but by listening to it, you made the decision your angels wanted you to make. This doesn't mean that something bad would've happened on the date; it could mean that the relationship or the person wasn't right for you at that time. It's important not to focus on the "why" when your intuition makes decisions for you. Instead, you just need to accept it and move on.
2. ***You'll feel connected and supported.*** Feeling support is necessary for your mental and emotional health. Your family, friends, and coworkers usually fulfill this need in the physical realm, but your spirit guides can help you in other ways. For example, you can have all the support you can ask for in life

but still feel incomplete. You might feel lost or that you don't know your mission in life. You try to convey your emotions to your family and friends, but they can't understand what you mean. In this instance, the higher powers are the only entities that can help reach your fulfillment, which you can only do when you connect with them.

3. *You'll receive clarity of your life's purpose.* Before you were born, your soul decided on your life's purpose, such as your career or using your skills to help other people. Throughout your life, you build on this purpose so that it's fulfilled once you cross over. It's easy to feel drawn to your purpose because it's a part of your heart. Therefore, you might have always felt the need to teach, or perhaps you're drawn to work in a nonprofit where you can help with counseling people who are struggling. However, sometimes you might be on the right track but still feel that something isn't right. You feel incomplete but don't understand why. Turning to the higher powers can help you understand where your life is lacking so your life's path becomes

clearer. You'll also begin to understand why certain events occur in your life, such as the sudden death of a loved one or losing a job.
4. *They help you overcome challenges.* It doesn't matter who you are, how much money you have, or how happy you are in life. You'll still have challenges that you need to overcome. Before, after, and during these troubling times, your spiritual entities are actively negotiating with other people's guides to help ensure that your problems are solved. It doesn't matter whether you're struggling financially, emotionally, or psychologically — your guides are on your side.
5. *The higher powers are here to protect you.* The physical and spiritual worlds are filled with good and bad entities. You have people who can hurt you on earth, and then there are evil spirits that can harm you spiritually. It doesn't matter what entity is trying to harm you or how — the higher powers know what's happening, and they will do everything in their power to ensure your safety. For example, if you feel that your home is filled with negative energy, call on your spirit guides to help you bring more

peace in your home. While they'll naturally try to erase negativity, they can only do so much unless you ask for their help.
6. ***You'll feel happier.*** One of the biggest changes that you'll feel is happiness. Even if you feel truly happy before you connect to your guides, the feeling will still increase as you strengthen communication. This happens because you don't just feel that you're heading the right direction to fulfill your mission — you know it. You feel more calm and relaxed even in the middle of chaos because you know that the entities are with you. You don't feel alone because you know you're never alone. You also have a different mindset that focuses on positive thoughts, bringing more positivity into your life.

Be Aware of Blocks

Blocking is when you can't get through to the higher powers. There are many reasons for blocks, such as not believing in your guides, and it's important that you investigate your reason so you can make the lines of communication clear again.

One of the biggest blocks is that you lack experience. This is common with people who are just starting to build the communication lines. You might dive into the research and think that you need to read as much as possible about the topic, but you really don't. All you need to do is take a step back and feel. Keep an open heart and mind so you can receive their messages. You have to break down your barriers by relaxing your mind and focusing on guided meditation.

Impatience is another block. It takes time to strengthen communication and to receive the messages. Patience is a key factor but also a personality trait where many people struggle. If you feel that your impatience is getting in the way of talking with your guides, focus on improving your patience. For example, you can become mindful of your impatience, and when you start to notice you're lacking, take a deep breath and count to 10. Another trick is to focus on taking your time. If you realize you work quickly, start slowing down your pace. Take a day wherein you specifically focus on nourishing your patience by making it a goal to keep this mindset at all times. Another way to reinforce this trait is to delay gratification. For instance, you want to nibble on a few potato chips while you're watching a movie. Instead of grabbing the chips at the beginning of the movie, see how long you can wait. Try to make it a goal to wait at least 15 minutes. Once you get to this point, try to go a little longer.

You can also have a block because of your expectations. For example, you think you're supposed to get some big sign that takes your breath away, which is rarely the case. Usually, your angels speak to you through little signs, such as seeing repeating numbers for a period of time, having a certain feeling, catching a fleeting visual, or hearing a whisper in your ear. They'll make sure to catch your attention for at least a second, but you might not think that it's a message from your angels right away. You might see the number 444 many times in a day, such as in the mileage of your car or the receipt from a grocery store. Then you might start to look at the clock whenever the time hits 4:44. You might also wake up at this time in the morning. It can take you a couple of weeks before you start to think it's a sign from above.

The food you eat is another block. What you put into your body can create an imbalance in your energy, which your guides need to converse with you. The healthier you eat, the better you'll feel, and this will make your energy increase. This means you have to limit your fast food intake. You also need to get enough fruits and vegetables into your diet. Try to stay away or limit the amount of soda you consume, and don't have an alcoholic drink when you want to reach out to your angels. Sugars, sweeteners, fatty meats, unhealthy oils, white rice, genetically modified food, and processed foods are also ones to eat rarely.

Another block is when you overanalyze. Your guides won't always connect with you when you're meditating; they might do it later in the day. You might even have several days when you meditate and don't get many signs from them, and then suddenly you're working and you have insight. This is the way they work, which is why you need to have faith in them. Overanalyzing can make you listen for every sound, keep your eyes looking all around the room, and make you lose the connection because you're not focused on your faith. When you start to feel that you're overanalyzing or becoming a little anxious, take a deep breath and relax your mind.

Tips for the Best Communication Experience

One of the best tips I can give is to keep a clear mind. You mustn't let the chaos of life cloud your mind. You won't receive the messages clearly if your mind isn't clear. You might even feel that you should look at the clock but decide to continue working, which can make you miss what the higher powers are trying to tell you. If you start to feel your thoughts racing, focus on a relaxation technique. For example, close your eyes and take a few deep and slow breaths. Another technique is to visualize a place that makes you feel calm, such as a meadow or waterfall.

Start communicating with an intention in your mind. Before you try guided meditation, ask yourself why you want to connect with your guides. Do you want to know what direction you should take in your career? Do you worry about your love life? Are you feeling lost and want to know why? It doesn't matter what question you have for your angels — they're ready to listen to you, and they will do what they can to answer your question. The key is to be clear about your intentions. Don't be afraid or ashamed of what you want to ask. There are no silly questions when it comes to your spirit guides.

Another tip is to train yourself to remember your dreams. You can do this by starting a dream journal, or work on remembering the main points as they'll help you fill in the blanks for the smaller details. It doesn't matter when you wake up during the night. Turn on your light, and write your dream down. You want to do this before you do anything else because the smaller details will leave your mind quickly.

It's important not to just jump into meditation. You want to start the process of guided meditation slowly and go at your pace. For example, you might start by looking for a quiet place in your home and staying there for a minute. Focus on the most comfortable spot to lie down or sit up. Then listen carefully to see if you can block out the noise that surrounds your home. If you feel that you can't remain focused in this spot, then find a different location. Once you've found the perfect area, start decorating it with items that make you feel at peace. You might have sounds of a waterfall, a place to listen to calming music, or a few candles. Take a couple of days to become used to your calm surroundings. Go sit in the area and take in the sights, smells, and sounds. Focus on becoming one with your chosen spot so that you don't find any surprises as you're trying to focus on communicating.

Every good relationship starts with a pleasant introduction, so start communicating by asking your guide for their name. Don't ask the question in your head — speak it loud and proud. All you need to do is ask, "To my guardian angel who is watching over me now, would you please say your name?" Use your intuition as you listen for their name. It might be a name that you've never heard of before. If the name feels right to you, write it down and believe it.

Differences and Similarities Between the Higher Powers

It's not surprising that many people become a little confused about the differences between all the higher powers, such as archangels, angels, guardian angels, and spirit guides. Part of this is because you can choose to believe what you want. Another part of this is because there's a lot of information in the world that doesn't match up. For instance, some books will refer to spirit guides as guardian angels, while other books will explain them as two separate entities. When you're starting to learn about the higher powers, this is confusing, and it can make you question whether it's a topic you want to dive into. Therefore, let me make it as clear as possible to you.

First, there are different levels of higher powers. For instance, the archangels are the most powerful angels, but for many religions and people, they're not the most powerful entities. Christians believe that God is the most powerful spirit and the archangels are below him. However, not everyone believes in God. Some people feel that there is another higher power, the leader of all the archangels, and that is Archangel Michael. They see him as the most powerful entity in the universe. You need to decide what you believe by listening to the words of your religion, your intuition, and your belief with the spiritual world. No one can tell you that you're right or wrong; you need to tell yourself.

Second, archangels and angels are protectors. They don't necessarily guide you in your day-to-day life because that's the job of your guardian angels. For instance, when you receive a sign from the angels, it's your guardian angels who ensure that you see and understand it.

Third, archangels, angels, and guardian angels are in constant communication with each other. They all work together to ensure that you get your message, but they also have their separate jobs. For example, archangels are the ones who speak to God. They receive a message for you from him. From there, the archangels communicate with the angels, who then inform your guardian angels of the message. At this point, it's up to the guardian angel to ensure that you get the message. This is when you'll start to see repeating numbers, hear voices, get a sensation in your gut, have a dream, or get an idea in your mind. Your guardian angels will continue to relay the message to you until you understand it.

However, just because the higher powers work together to give you messages doesn't mean they have the same job. In the next chapter, you'll learn that there are seven main archangels, and they each have different powers and jobs. For instance, Archangel Ariel is associated with Mother Earth and nature. Therefore, when your message from God is about nature, he'll call up Ariel to relay the message to one of the angels she watches over, and then that angel will go to one of your guardian angels.

Fourth, when it comes to angels that work to keep you safe, you have at least one and up to three. They'll stay with you throughout your life. When it comes to your guardian angels, you can have several. Guardian angels tend to come and go throughout your life, usually only staying for a certain time frame or life lesson. For example, one guardian angel will watch over you when you're sleeping, and another one will come once you wake up. You might have another guardian step in when you're going through the death of a loved one because their specialty is to help you get through your grief. This means that your guardians will leave you if you don't need them. However, you always have a few guardian angels at your side.

Fifth, when it comes to angels, they need your permission to help you. This means you need to call them directly. You can do this by calling their name or simply asking your angels to help you. Your guardians don't need permission to help you because this is their job.

Sixth, you've probably heard that when a loved one passes on, they become an angel. This isn't true because angels don't usually take human form. However, guardian angels often take the form of humans, and they can be your loved ones that passed on. Some of your guardians might also be one of your ancestors, such as your great-great-grandma. They can also be souls that you've known from a past life, providing you believe in reincarnation.

COMMON QUESTIONS

Do angels have their own names?

Yes, all archangels, angels, and guardians have their own names. Sometimes you might recognize the name when you hear it — especially if you're talking to one of your guardians — because it's the name of your grandfather or great-grandmother.

How do you know you're really communicating with them?

You need to listen to your body. You'll feel it when you're communicating with them. You also need to believe it. You might have a little voice in your head telling you that "it's not true," but if you truly feel in your gut that it is, don't listen to that little voice.

Do you need to worry about something else (e.g., negative spirits or ghosts) communicating with you instead?

You don't need to worry about a negative entity communicating with you, but you need to be aware that it can happen. As long as you pay attention to the signs and your intuition, you'll be fine. If you're trying to talk to one of your guardian angels and hear a voice but your gut makes you feel like something isn't right, you need to stop the communication. Try to notice if you have any blocks that are keeping your angels from coming through, or try calling them directly when you have a clearer mind.

What type of questions should I ask my angels?

You can ask your angels any question you have, but be prepared that you might not get an answer, especially right away. Asking your angels questions isn't like asking eight-ball questions. Your angels won't ignore a question, but they might be trying to give you a message that's more important and unrelated to your question.

What is guided meditation?

This is when you meditate but you receive instructions on how to perform your meditation. For example, in this book, I've provided a script that will help you follow your meditation procedure. A meditation audiobook can also help you with this process. You can also perform guided meditation through therapy sessions.

2

ARCHANGELS AND GUIDED MEDITATION

An archangel is the angel of the highest rank and holds the most power among the angels. The term is found in a number of religious texts and states they were created by God at the dawn of time. Along with being his messengers, they're also meant to serve God. All archangels are spiritual beings who have never had a human life. Some people believe that sometimes they'll take the form of a human when they're called upon to help. However, they're powerful enough that they can help humans without taking human form.

SEVEN MAIN ARCHANGELS

Surveys show that over 80 percent of the world's populations believe in angels and usually think of archangels instead of any other spiritual being (Demers, n.d.). No one really knows the true number of archangels, and there are various numbers when you start reading about the main archangels. Below, I will discuss the seven main archangels, as this is the most common number in research. As you continue growing spiritually, you'll learn that some people claim there are only four, while others feel there are over a dozen. I encourage you to look through this research when you come across it because it's the best way to form your belief system.

1. Archangel Michael is known as the Warrior Angel. His name means "he who is a god," and he is seen as the most powerful angel. He is seen not only as a leader and protector but also as the patron angel of justice, righteousness, and mercy. He can give your confidence, support, courage, direction, energy, motivation, self-esteem, and he can help you find your life's purpose. Some people will pray to him over God or another higher power, especially when they're afraid, concerned for their safety, going into battle, confused, or in need of spiritual assistance.

Because Michael is a warrior, he is shown with a sword and sometimes in gear that represents war. This gives him a bold personality, which is exactly how he'll communicate with you. One of the biggest signs that help you know that Archangel Michael is near you is hearing his voice. It's one that you can't ignore. He has the clearest and loudest voice of all the angels. He will speak to you bluntly, which can make people feel that he is yelling orders at them or that he is bossy. He uses this voice to get your attention so you can listen to his words. Once he knows that you hear him, his voice will change so you feel that it's full of compassion. Michael has just as much love for you as all other angels. He even has a sense of humor that he uses to help guide you.

Another sign that Archangel Michael is near you is that you'll start to feel peace surround you. His voice is known to make you feel calm so you can start to think and act clearly in times of crisis. If you ever believe that Michael is trying to communicate with you, but you feel guilt, emptiness, or another emotion that drains you, it's time to push your ego aside and open your mind and heart to Michael.

Michael will always make you feel protected even when you're afraid. If you're in a situation wherein you're anxious or scared but you also have an intense feeling of peace and that someone is protecting you, Archangel Michael is at your side. This is because Michael embraces you with his large wings, making you feel his energy as strongly as possible.

Even though you need to call on Archangel Michael to help you, he can stay with you for as long as you feel necessary. All you need to do is ask him to stay with you. You can call on Michael through guided meditation or by saying a prayer. Michael is the only archangel that's mentioned in three major religions, so he has several common prayers. You can also use guided meditation, or you can ask him to come to you in your dreams by inviting him. Simply say before you go to bed, "Archangel Michael, please connect with me in my dreams."

2. *Archangel Raphael* is referred to as the Healing Angel because his name means "God heals." His focus is to help you heal in every aspect of your life. He also works closely with people who are in the healing profession, such as doctors, psychologists, and ministers. If you feel that you're struggling when it comes to healing, you can call on Raphael to help you through guided meditation or by asking him to help heal you through this time.

Raphael is the archangel you'll call upon when you're trying to overcome addiction. He will guide you through your recovery and will embrace you when you ask him to help you through a craving or when you feel weak. If you're sick with a cold or were just diagnosed with a life-threatening illness, know that Raphael is on your side.

He is also the angel who watches over you as you travel to help you have a safe and happy journey. He can also help you restore harmony and peace in your life, as well as fight any illness or disease that is plaguing you or your family.

You'll know that Archangel Raphael is on your side because you'll see sparkles of green, which is his color. You can call on his energy to surround you by visualizing a bright-green light all around your body. Close your eyes and imagine a green light coming down from the universe. It encircles you, starting from the top of your head and working its way down to your feet. It goes all around you, so no matter where you go, you'll have this light with you. Green is a warm color, so don't be surprised if you start to feel a warm sensation throughout your body during your visualization.

Another sign is by seeing his name appear to you in random places. Raphael isn't shy, so he doesn't mind giving you messages through bold or large letters and numbers. These signs will usually show up once you've requested Raphael's assistance and you feel like you're at the end of your rope. It's his way to let you know that he hears you and that he is right next to you. Now, it's up to you to continue to have faith and connect with him more as he'll continue to help guide you. Like Archangel Michael, Raphael also has a sense of humor, and it can show up through signs. For example, if you request his assistance and you see a book fly off the shelf in front of you and it puts a smile on your face, this is Raphael.

3. Archangel Gabriel is often called the Messenger Angel. She is the only female archangel mentioned in the Bible, and her name means "God is my strength." She is the angel that helps you when you're trying to give the world your messages, whether they're through music, writing, teaching, or another means. She helps you find motivation so you can focus on your skills to get these messages to other people, even if it's just in your classroom.

If you're struggling to overcome your fear of communicating with people, whether it's talking over the phone or giving a presentation, Gabriel is here to help you. All you need to do is call her as you're preparing, and then ask her to guide you through this process. She's also the angel who surrounds women and children, especially during times of conceptions, pregnancy, and childbirth.

One sign to know that Archangel Gabriel is with you is when you notice any gold or white light. You might see this light in your mind's eye or physically. You might even look toward an item in your home that's white or gold and then feel a sensation in you, letting you know that she's with you. Other signs are hearing a trumpet and seeing a feather. You can also simply feel Gabriel's energy around you and know that it's her.

4. Archangel Jophiel is known as the Angel of Beauty. Her name means "beauty of God," and her mission is to help you see everything that's beautiful in your life. She's the angel that will help you focus on positive thoughts. When you're struggling or feeling overly stressed, you can call on Jophiel, and you'll start to see yourself looking out at nature, up to the sky, or watching your family and smile because you get this feeling that life is peaceful and you're lucky. You might even see a picture on your phone and think about how beautiful it looks. It's this feeling that lets you know Archangel Jophiel is with you.

Jophiel is the archangel who watches over artists. She helps them create beautiful works of art that help people feel calm and happy, and she gives the world a sense of peace. If you're compelled to draw a heart, it's a sign that she's with you.

She will also help people tame their egos, especially if it's getting in the way of your mission and seeing the greatness in the world. By making you more grounding, Archangel Jophiel can help you see the world through a different lens. You'll also notice the smaller parts of your life that are there to help you smile and give order to the chaos.

5. Archangel Ariel, also written as Uriel, is called the Angel of Nature and Animals. Many people call her the patron saint of animals as her name means "lion or lioness of God." She oversees the protection and growth of animals, nature, and the earth. She's also the archangel who helps veterinarians, as well as people who focus on helping the environment. If your animals are ill or your community is in a drought, it's best to contact Ariel as she'll work to help everything through the difficult times. She works closely with Archangel Raphael whenever there's an illness in nature or animals.

When you want to learn more about nature or go exploring, seek the assistance of Ariel. She can also guide you when you are preparing for a hike. Ask her to follow you along your journey as she'll protect not only your surroundings but also you. Ariel is also known to help you reach your full potential. She can help you strengthen your psychic abilities, discover nature's secrets, increase clairvoyance, and inspire you with new ideas and inventions.

One of the main signs that Ariel is near you is that you'll feel inspired by nature. You might be walking outside and notice how green the grass has gotten and become happy, thinking about spring and the warmer weather ahead. You might feel down and drive by a lake or a landscape that takes your breath away.

6. Archangel Azrael is referred to as the Angel of Death. His name means "whom God helps," and there is no reason to fear his main purpose, which is to help you transition from the physical world to the spiritual realm. He also helps souls to adjust to the spirit world after death, along with your loved ones who are still grieving on the physical plane. Azrael is the angel who comes to you when you request assistance for your grieving. He works closely with grief counselors, ministers, and many other people who assist you after losing a loved one.

Azrael will also help you transition when you're trying to end a part of your life. For example, if you're struggling with graduating after high school, call on Archangel Azrael because he will help you. If you're trying to stay sober after fighting drug addiction, Azrael is on your side. He wants the process to go smoothly, so he won't leave your side until he knows that you'll be okay.

The energy you feel from Azrael is one of the biggest signs that he's near you. Even when you're struggling with grief, you'll feel a sense of hope. You'll feel that there is a strong, stoic, respectful, and quiet presence around you. You'll find yourself remembering all the good times with your loved one and laughing. You might tell yourself that you know everything will be okay. Your inner strength will start to grow, and this lets you know that Azrael has heard your calls.

7. Archangel Chamuel is also known as the Angel of Peaceful Relationships. His name can also be spelled

Khamuel, Camniel, Cameel, and Camiel, and it means "he who sees God." His main mission is to focus on making the world a peaceful place. He is often around when you see a negative turn into a positive. You also know he's with you when you see a horrible event unfold on the television but you feel that everything will be all right because of all the people helping. You'll notice the heroes in the story instead of the villains.

You can call on Chamuel when you feel like there is too much negativity in your life, whether it's internal or external, and he'll help you change your mindset. When you're struggling with anxiety, you can call on him, and he'll guide you and let you know that you're not alone. Through his messages and energy, he'll show you how to overcome your anxiety or negativity and help you reach your full potential.

If you have an item that's lost, you can call on Archangel Chamuel to help you find it. You can also ask him to help you find a piece of you that's lost. For instance, if you're at a crossroads in your life and not sure which path to take, he can guide you.

One of the biggest ways you know that Chamuel is with you is your growing confidence or self-esteem.

Even if you're about to give a presentation and you're shy or struggle with social anxiety, he'll help you feel calm and give you the courage to face your fears.

Archangels and Guided Meditation

Unlike other angels, you need to call archangels for help through prayers or ask for their guidance. Archangels might know that you need help, but they can't send you energies or help you unless you reach out to them directly. Because each archangel has their specific jobs, you can find prayers related to them. However, you can always send each one of them a simple message that requests their assistance. For example, if you're fighting an illness, you can say, "Archangel Raphael, please guide me during my time of illness and heal me with your powers. Thank you."

It's always important to remain pleasant while requesting assistance from your archangels. It doesn't mean they'll help you faster or they'll ignore you if you're not polite. It's a way to start out in a compassionate tone and help you receive their messages easier. Remember, a clear mind is key when you're trying to communicate with your higher powers.

EXAMPLE GUIDED MEDITATION SCRIPT

In this meditation, you can call in any archangel you feel you need, but I'll focus on calling Ariel.

> *Find a comfortable, quiet place to lie down or sit. Find your breath and notice as it slowly moves into a comfortable rhythm. Place one hand on top of your heart as the pulse of the universe aligns with your heart chakra. As you feel your hand move with your breath, feel your tension start moving away from your heart, down toward your stomach, legs, and then out through your feet. Imagine the tension soaring through the air, further and further away from you.*
>
> *Continue to breathe normally as your muscles start to relax. Let your limbs fall to where they please as you allow the calm and peaceful environment to connect with you. Your aura is clear, clean, and white as it gently and slowly starts to expand out into the area. You feel the walls and all the physical items*

that surround you blend in as you become aware of the angels that surround you every day. You feel yourself become one with the universe as your lines of connection flow open a little farther.

Ask the Archangel Ariel to make herself known as you feel the warm sensations of your body. Your room starts to fill with a gorgeous pink hue of light as Ariel comes closer to your physical body. The other angels start to step back as you continue to feel her light of support and love surround you. You start to recognize her energy of compassion and love. You start to feel her energy and personality, and she becomes clearer to you as you notice a difference between Ariel and other energies that surround you.

You start to feel her soft pink light connecting with your heart chakra. You feel them connect through the rhythm with the thumping of your heart. The vibrations of her energy and your heart are now in unison as you continue to connect with the lovely Ariel.

When you feel completely loved and supported, ask the Archangel Ariel to present any messages she has. Ask her to present them to you from the highest good, knowing that you'll receive the messages with high clarity.

Let yourself feel these messages and energy as it glides through your body, filling your heart and soul with love and pink light. Keep the connection until you feel that you're full of the energies that Ariel is sharing with you. Start bringing yourself back to your physical world slowly by becoming aware of your whole spiritual team. Bring your aura in, closer to your body. Take a deep breath and close your chakras to a level where you're comfortable. They're now grounded and clean so you can start bringing your aura fully back into your physical body, starting from your head and going all the way to your toes.

Take a breath and start wiggling your fingers and toes. Feel the light and love from the physical world as you slowly start opening your eyes. You're getting ready to take on the rest of the day. Once you're ready, slowly get up and allow your feet to meet with the floor. Stand straight as you allow the vibrations of the physical world to come back into your body.

3

ANGELS AND GUIDED MEDITATION

Just like archangels have their own roles, so do other angels. The only difference is archangels don't usually share their responsibilities with other archangels, but angels will share their duties. For example, you have more than one angel that helps keep you safe every day of your life. They work together to ensure that you're protected while your guardian angels guide you. This is a duty that they share, and they work closely with your guardians to ensure that you're on the right path for your life. Even when you're struggling, feeling lost, or not reaching your full potential, the angels and guardian angels are still working together because they have faith in you. They know that you can follow their lead and fulfill your life's mission.

TYPES OF ANGELS

You can think of angels as the overseers of the world. You can even imagine that they are in the sky looking down on everyone and everything as you go about your day. This thought can often help you feel at peace and a part of the universe when you're starting to feel lost.

The angels work closely with the archangels, who oversee and help them when needed. Just like there are different archangels, there are different types of angels. The important difference to remember is that each type of angel holds dozens of angels. For example, there are dozens or possibly hundreds of helper angels in the universe, but there is only one Archangel Michael.

1. Helper angels are experts in pretty much every field in the universe. For example, if you need help choosing a college, you can call on a helper angel. If you need help buying your first house, you can ask a helper angel to join your realtor team. You can call on helper angels to assist you with anything in your life. These angels don't tend to stick to you for very long because they tend to soar around the universe and help whoever needs their help. When you ask for a helper angel, they'll stay with you until the project is completed, at which time it's best to thank them for their help as then they know they can comfortably move on to the next person.

2. Power angels can help you when you need more power, whether it's emotional, psychological, physical, or spiritual. They know that you're a powerful being, and they want to make sure that you realize your full potential through your power. When you struggle with setting boundaries, it's time to contact one of these angels, as they can help you learn how to reinforce your boundaries. Power angels also remind you that you have unique qualities to help reach your life's purpose. They tend to send you into challenging situations, but there's no need to worry because they'll also see you through to the end.

3. Peace angels are a group of angels that come to you when you need to get through a difficult chapter in your life. You don't need to feel that your life is falling apart or full of chaos. You don't need to wait until you feel you need peace in your life to call on them — your heart and soul can feel at peace and still call a peace angel. They can also help you get through the death of a loved one, a challenging transition, or an illness. They walk with you as you face the music and then stay with you until you feel that the end has come. Sometimes they'll give you good memories or make you feel inspired so you can pick up the pieces and move on. If you're struggling with something in your life — from financial issues to emotional problems — call on a peace angel, and they will help you.

4. Star angels believe that the sky's the limit, and they want to see you reach your dreams. If you wished upon a star as a child and kept this magic within you, you're closest to the star angels, and you believe in them. When you wished on a star and it came true, it's because of these angels. The purpose of a star angel is to help you manifest your soul's dreams so you can fulfill your life's mission. You can call on one of these angels when you're working toward a goal, and they'll stay with you until you thank them for your help, even if your goal takes years to complete. There is no timeframe in the universe, and there are plenty of star angels to help everyone else.

5. Flower angels work closely with Archangel Ariel because they help care for nature, especially the flowers. They'll help you realize the beauty around you, especially when you feel emotionally down or worried about nature. For example, if you know that there are wetlands that are in danger, take time to ask the flower angels for help as you try to preserve the lands. When a flower angel feels that you need more beauty in your life, they'll inspire you to go out in nature for a walk, observe your horizons, or build a garden. If you're an artist, you might feel compelled to draw a landscape. Flower angels will help you reach your full potential by ensuring you remember to take time to focus on the beauty surrounding you and take care of your planet.

6. Angels of mercy are by yourself when you feel hopeless, worthless, or depressed. When you reach a point where you don't think you can continue, it's time to call the angels of mercy. They're often found in places where people struggle the most, such as hospitals, the battlefield, and areas under a state of calamity. However, they also help those who are struggling with poverty, abuse, and any other problem. Even if you feel it's minor, an angel of mercy will help you through once they're called. Think of these angels as the first responders of the spirit world because they'll rush to you just like the police, firefighters, or paramedics. Even though they can't always change the event, they'll do what they can to make you feel more at peace and guide you through tough times.

*7. **Messenger angels*** are the ones who spend their time making sure you get the messages you need from God or the archangels. Even though all angels give messages, these angels have a duty to carry special messages to you. Messenger angels won't stay with you very long. In fact, they move faster than the speed of light with the message and will pop it into your mind. For example, if you're working and suddenly a thought comes into your mind to call your dad, this is from a messenger angel. You can call on these angels to help send messages to other humans or even spirits in heaven. For instance, you can ask a messenger angel to let your dad know that you love him, and they'll bring this message to him in a flash.

*8. **Abundance angels*** are who you call on when you want more of something, such as time, value, purpose, or money. It's important to note that you shouldn't use angels in greedy or negative means. They usually won't answer your prayers when you ask for something that you really don't need, but they might give you something else that's special. For example, you might ask for a better financial future but get more time with your family. This is because the angel who helped you felt that more money wouldn't help you in your life. They felt what you really needed was more time with your family and yourself. You can also call on these angels to help your friends in need, and they'll follow through as well as they can.

9. Healing angels work closely with Archangel Raphael. You call on them when you need healing in your journey. It doesn't matter if it's physical, emotional, mental, or spiritual — they'll help you in any way they can. You don't need to call healing angels to help you. For example, if you're heading to the doctor's office or you're sick, one of them is right by your side. To get the most out of healing angels, call on to them to help you heal pieces of yourself. You don't need to direct them to a certain piece of your journey because they know where you need healing the most.

How Angels Communicate With You

It's important to pay attention to communication from the angels as it's essential for guided meditation. You can use the messages you receive from them to ask them for clarity. For example, if you understand angel numbers and they're telling you that your thoughts are manifesting, you can ask them a question about this. Maybe you want to know what thoughts are manifesting and if you should look toward your career or personal life.

Angel numbers are one of the main ways they communicate with you. When you see a repetitive number sequence often, it's the angels trying to communicate with you. Every single digit means something special in the spiritual world, and the meaning increases with each additional number. For example, angel number 1 reminds you that the angels are connected to your thoughts so you need to be mindful of what you're thinking. Angel number 11 reminds you to focus on positive thoughts and start removing the negativity from your life, such as toxic thoughts or people. Angel number 111 means that you need to start having persistent positive thoughts towards the direction you want. For instance, if you want to build your writing career, focus your thoughts and work on this. Angel number 1111 tells you that your thoughts are now manifesting and these thoughts go back all the way to angel number 1.

Angels will also communicate with you by showing you animal symbols. These work similar to numbers, as each symbol means something important in the spiritual world. If you start to notice a symbol showing up repeatedly, it's time to do a little research so that you can obtain your message or get clarity.

You can even use your social media accounts to get messages through your angels. While they don't have an account, they might ensure that you see a certain article or post so you can get the message they have for you. It's always possible to get their messages from other people, just as you can ask them to give messages to other people.

Angels will make you feel a certain way when they have a message for you. The energies you feel in your body don't lie, so pay attention. For example, if you suddenly feel a little chilled, you have to observe what's going on around you and ask your angel for clarity of your message. However, some sensations are common knowledge. For instance, feeling a bad sensation or having butterflies in your stomach is your intuition telling you that something isn't right. If you're about to take a drive or tell someone that you'll go on a date with them, you should probably think twice and say no. Ringing in your ears is also a sign from your angels. Usually, this means that your instinctive thought before or during the ringing is part of your message.

Angels also communicate to us by leaving us feathers, coins, or other signs. They give us symbolic dreams or let us smell fragrances that suddenly appear and you can't explain. There are dozens of ways that they communicate, so it's important to become mindful of your surroundings, and take note when you feel that something you hear, see, smell, feel, or taste might be a sign from an angel.

ANGELS AND GUIDED MEDITATION

Mindfulness is important when you're using guided meditation. You want to ensure that as you allow your aura to go through the spiritual plane. Remain mindful. For instance, you don't want to have negative thoughts, and you need to avoid thinking about all the tasks you need to do on that day, as these things can cause stress and distract you while you are trying to communicate spiritually. Distracting thoughts can become a block and cause you to miss the message from the angel.

If you find your thoughts wandering while you're trying to communicate, take a step back, and focus on mindful meditation first. Throughout your day, you can practice mindfulness, such as noticing landmarks as you drive or thinking about the action you're taking when you perform a task.

One important thing to remember when using guided meditation to talk to your angels is that they might not leave once the meditation is over. If you call the healing angels to help you heal your anxiety, they'll stay with you for a while as they continue to guide you through your triggers that cause your anxiety to grow. The key is you want to stay in the meditation long enough so you can feel your energy start to heal.

> *Start the guided meditation process by finding a quiet, comfortable location, such as your bedroom, office, or living room. It should be a place where you can let your mind rest and focus on meditating. This may mean that you need to find a way to block out the sound of children or set your pets in another part of your home so that they don't bother you mid-meditation.*
> *Once you've selected your location, lie down and close your eyes. As you focus on your breathing, call out your angels. If you know their name, call their name. If you want to request a certain*

group of angels, such as the healing angels, say, "Healing angels of the universe, please come to me to help me heal the worry I feel." If you want them to heal something specific in your life, such as your anxiety, cold, or the grief of losing a loved one, you can ask them to heal you in this way by saying, "Please heal the anxiety that I feel in my body during the day. Please help increase my confidence and strength within me. Help me know that you are with me along my life's journey."

You will then start to focus on your normal breathing. Once your mind and body are in a relaxed state, take several deep, slow breaths. Slowly inhale through your nose, keeping your mouth closed. When you exhale, slightly open your lips to allow the air to release from your body slowly. Here's a tip: if you're having trouble feeling relaxed, imagine your tense energy leaving your body as you breathe out. You can visualize a black cloud of air. When you inhale, imagine the clean, fresh, relaxing, and positive air around you entering your body.

Once you start to feel that your mind is at ease and your limbs are heavy with relaxation, move on to the next step of visualizing a white light slowly surrounding your body. The light comes from the earth and starts to connect you to the angels. This light is the energy from the angels you are calling.

Continue to focus on the light moving through your body from your feet and out the top of your head. Then, the light covers your body like a blanket. Focus on the light from your angels and feel your body becoming stronger as they connect. This light will continue to spread through your body, giving you sensations of love, warmth, and energy.

Once you feel the energy from the angels, you may end the meditation by saying, "Thank you for your help and guidance." Then start bringing yourself back into reality by imagining the white light slowly moving from your body. Once the light is gone, begin to sense your body. Start by wiggling your fingers and toes. Notice the rhythm of your breathing and the aroma of your room. Slowly open your eyes and look up toward your ceiling as you continue to move your body. Once you feel your sensations, slowly get up and continue with your day.

Now that you understand the process, it's time to get comfortable and start the guided meditation.

Lie down, make yourself comfortable, and close your eyes. Call on the angels you wish to connect with by asking for their help. In your mind, ask the angels to come and heal your worries. Focus on your normal breathing. Breathe in, breathe out, breathe in, breathe out. Breathe deeply in through your nose and out through your mouth as you release your worries, tension, and anxiety. Your muscles become relaxed as the tension leaves your body with each exhale. Focus on your breath. Slowly breathe in and out, in and out.

Without changing the rhythm of your breath, notice each breath as you breathe in and out. You're starting to connect with the flow of your breath.

Feel the softness of your body as it becomes heavier. Notice your breath becoming slower. Now, breathe down to your feet. Take time to relax them. Imagine roots going from your feet deep into the earth. The roots are going deep into the dirt, rocks, and sand. Let your roots drink up the white energy from the earth up to your feet, spreading the light into your toes, heels, ankles, legs, and up the rest of your body. Feel the energy slowly spreading into every cell and muscle as they become more relaxed with the massaging of the light. Let the light spread further up your body, into your hips, lower back, and stomach. Allow the light to soothe your aches and pains as it continues to your upper back, shoulder blades, neck, and into your mind. The energy of the light relaxes and clears your mind.

Let the light flow from the top of your head

and down the outside of your body. Feel it cover your face, throat, and slowly down your chest. Allow the light to spread over your arms and down your abdomen, hips, legs, and ankles. Feel the warmth of the light as it spreads over your feet, covering your whole body like a warm, loving, and healing blanket.

Feel the light grow with healing energy as you call forth your angels. Continue to feel the energy of the light that surrounds you as you see another ball of white light glowing brightly. Watch the light come down from the sky as it becomes bigger, taller, and brighter. As the angel comes closer, you feel the warmth of their light. You feel their energy as they strengthen the light surrounding your body. Allow the angel to come closer and closer to you, gliding down from the universe and toward your energy. Feel the energy from the angel and your energy connect. Let the light become brighter and brighter as it starts moving into your body, filling you with healing energy.

Thank the angels for their energy and slowly start bringing the light back through your body. The light surrounding you becomes dimmer as it soaks into your body. The roots connecting your feet to the earth start to curl back up and into your body. The healing energy remains inside of you as the roots completely vanish back into your body. You're now bringing your mind back to reality. Slowly, you start to smell the aroma of the room. You hear the sounds that help bring you back from your meditative state. You begin to feel your limbs. Wiggle your fingers and toes as your sensations continue to bring you back.

Notice the rhythm of your breathing as you slowly open your eyes and allow them to settle with the light surrounding your room. Continue lying until you feel the strength enter your muscles. Stretch your body before you sit up and return to your day.

4

GUARDIAN ANGELS AND GUIDED MEDITATION

No matter where you go or what you do, you always have guardian angels next to you. Aside from guiding you and doing what they can to protect you from harm, they also pray for you. They want to ensure that your prayers are answered, so they communicate with other higher powers and use their energies in their prayers. Some faiths believe that these angels record everything you say and think. This information is then passed on to other spiritual entities and brought into the universe to help your physical body and soul grow.

You should know that guardian angels choose you. Before you were born, they took a vow to protect, guide, and serve you. This is why your guardians are so devoted to you. It's important to take time every day to appreciate all the higher powers — especially your guardian angels — because they're constantly working hard for your best interest.

How Guardian Angels Communicate With You

In many ways, all higher powers communicate in the same way, but your guardian angels have their own special ways, and this can be different for each person. If you're not yet strong on your spiritual path, your guardian angels will give you messages in bold ways so you know that they're around. For example, if you understand angel numbers, they'll focus on this method. As you develop on your spiritual journey, the methods can change.

Your signs will come from everywhere. You might find yourself walking by a table and suddenly three papers fall on the floor. You pick them up and blame a breeze that came through the window or yourself, but this could be from your guardians. Take a look at the papers when this happens. Observe your thoughts. What answers have you been searching for from the higher powers? Is there anything on the paper that connects to you?

If you feel a random tingling sensation in your skin, pay attention — it's a common guardian angel sign.

You might feel positivity from this feeling, and it's common to see other signs, such as feathers, angel numbers, or voices.

Your angels will communicate with you through clouds. For example, you're driving to work and you see a cloud that reminds you of an angel. You take this as a sign that they're with you so there's no need to worry about your day ahead.

Years ago, I noticed that the songs on my iPod would stop in the middle and randomly go to another song. I thought the reasoning was a poor device, but then I started noticing connections between my thoughts and the music. I then realized that when the songs changed, it was a sign from my angels. They were trying to communicate with me about the thought I was having. Angels will communicate with you through music you hear (like what I experienced) or songs that pop into your head. You should take a moment to note the lyrics that repeat like a broken record in your mind and analyze them so you can see whether there's any connection between your life, emotions, and the music.

It's said that there is a rainbow every time it rains, but have you noticed that you only see them during certain times? The reason is that rainbows are a sign from your angels telling you that they've heard your prayers and they're working hard to help you make them a reality. They want you to remain focused and keep working toward your goal.

Guardian angels are our biggest communicators. They don't need us to call upon them because it's their job to guide us. However, you still need to take time to meditate and call on your guides as they can help you every day, not just when you feel you need them. For example, you're driving home in bad weather and start to worry about your safety. You take a moment to pray to your guardians that they'll get you and your family home safely. When you pull into your driveway, you take a deep breath and thank them for helping you get home. This doesn't mean that something bad would've happened if you didn't pray, because they're always protecting you. However, since you communicated with them, they knew that you wanted a little extra care during your drive.

Reaching out to your guardian angels to help you gives them more freedom to assist you. They're constantly busy buzzing around you to try to make your life easier, but this doesn't mean they know directly what you need. They can use their energies to connect with you and gather ideas, but communicating with them will make the process go smoother.

Another important reason why you need to reach out is that you have free will. No matter what your higher powers say or want you to do, you have the power to do whatever you choose. If you're at a crossroads in your job and have a feeling you should stay (which is what your guardian angels are trying to tell you to do) but you leave, they need to accept your decision. They don't become disappointed. Instead, they work on changing your path so you can continue to reach your life's mission.

EXAMPLE GUIDED MEDITATION SCRIPT

Before you begin meditating, find a comfortable and quiet place. You want to feel connected to this place so that it gives you a sense of peace and harmony. You can light candles and put on low, soothing, relaxing music to help your mind and body connect with your guardian angels on a deeper level.

If you know the name of one of your guardian angels, call them forth before you begin meditating. If you don't, close your eyes and ask, "I call forth the guardian angel ready to connect with me now. Please state your name." Listen to the first name that comes to your mind, no matter what it is, as this is the angel who will connect with you during your meditation. After you receive the name, proceed to tell the angel what you want them to help you with, such as understanding a message they're trying to give you.

When you're connecting with your guardian angel, focus on your breathing. Release all the negative energy in your body as this can damage any connection. When you breathe out, the negativity will leave your body. When you breathe in, the peace and harmony surrounding the room will fill your body.

Continue connecting with your guardian angel on a deeper level. Imagine their light making the room brighter as your energy starts to glow with it. When they've connected to you, now it's time to accept their energy. Notice the emotions you feel as you connect with them and any thoughts that pop into your mind as these are messages from your guardian angel.

When you feel the energy and messages are fulfilled, thank your angel for their assistance. You will then notice their light slowly backing away, becoming a little dimmer. Any light surrounding you will soak into your body and flow through your veins and into your cells, creating a feeling of peace and love. Then, you will slowly start to bring yourself back to reality before carrying on with your day.

Now that you know the process of connecting with your guardian angels, it's time to begin your meditation.

Start by finding a comfortable place to lie down and take a slow, deep breath. Slowly breathe in through your nose and out through your mouth. Start feeling your body's sensations as you begin to relax. Your muscles start to release their tensions as your limbs relax. Take another slow, deep breath in and then release. As you release your breath, imagine all the tension leaving your body. It starts sliding down from your head to your heart, through your legs, and out your feet. Imagine this tension flowing out through the window and into the universe, which will then transform it into positive energy.

Focus on replacing the negative energy that was in your body with peaceful and positive energy from the universe. Take a deep breath and imagine this energy flowing through your nose and into your body. As you breathe out, the energy slides into your heart, up to your head, and down to your feet.

Now, slowly bring your attention back to your relaxed breath. Allow your breathing to fall into a rhythm. Feel this rhythm as you begin to connect it with the energy around you. When the energies are synced, you'll start to see a white light. The dim light gradually

*becomes brighter as it moves
toward you.*

*Notice the feelings you receive from this
light. Feel the warmth on your face and
then covering the rest of your body.
Allow the love, compassion, and
positive emotions from this light to
surround you. Every breath you take,
you bring some of this energy into your
system. Now, you're surrounded by the
energies of your guardian angels inside
and outside of your body.*

*Let your aura feel the energies as it
connects deeper with the light. Allow
the connection to strengthen by
focusing on the energies of the light.
You're now connected with your
guardian angels. It's time to allow
yourself to become one with them. Let
them embrace you with their wings,
hold your hand, and send you their
energies.*

*Once the energies from the angels have
filled your body,*
*slowly bring your mind and body back to
your physical environment. You'll see*

the light become a bit dimmer, but it'll never fade away. Start wiggling your fingers and toes as you start noticing the sensations of your body again. Bring your mind back to your heartbeat as you start focusing on your breathing. Stay relaxed as you slowly bring yourself back from a meditative state.

Open your eyes slowly and look around your room. Connect yourself with the physical world before you sit up. Feel the floor beneath your feet, and wiggle your toes again. If you have carpet, notice how it feels on your feet. Gradually stand up and take a deep breath as you continue on with your day.

5

LOOKING INTO YOUR FUTURE

With all the information you've acquired in a short amount of time, it's easy to have some unanswered questions. Some of these questions are answered through your guardian angels or other higher powers as you continue to improve communication with them. Other questions you'll find answers through your intuition and simply what you come to believe. For example, I've talked to a lot of people about angel meditation and how to communicate, and sometimes they ask me, "But how do you know?" And I have to reply, "I just know." It's a thought I have, and my intuition tells me it's real, so I believe.

One of the most common questions you might have

is "Are there other higher powers that I can connect with?"

The short answer is yes. There are several other higher powers that you can try to connect with, but you should start with the three laid out in this book. From there, you should look toward your spirit guides, which you might notice are sometimes referred to as your guardian angels.

Spirit guides used to be living beings. They might have been your pets, parents, or friends. They have reached a certain point in their spiritual evolution, so they can stay to assist you. They might also come down from heaven or another realm to help you through a difficult time. They work closely with your guardian angels because they understand the challenges of being a human better than the angels. Most spirit guides will leave your side by the time you've reached adulthood, but you can still call them to help you through meditation and by requesting their assistance.

Another common question is "Is there a certain process I need to follow when I'm trying to communicate?"

No, there is no specific process. You can even meditate in different ways and still communicate with the higher powers. The only process you need to follow is the one that feels right for you. For example, if you feel that you can understand your guardian angel by closing your eyes and imagining them coming to you, then this is your process. You don't need to take the time to find a quiet place to meditate.

I've also been asked, "Do I need to believe in God and heaven to believe in angels?"

The short answer to this is no. You can believe in angels without believing in any other higher power. Some people believe in angels because they're referenced in the Bible, while some believe because they feel them. There are also people who focus on the energies of the universe, and they believe in angels as part of the universe's energy.

Finally, I will leave you with this question: "When will I know when I've learned enough about the higher powers?"

In answering this question, I find myself following my belief system that *you're never done learning* — not even when you've passed on from the physical world and find yourself soaring through the spiritual realm. You continue to grow and learn. If you believe in reincarnation, you might learn for your next life. You're also learning so you can strengthen your energies and continue to communicate between the two realms.

Continuing Your Communication

The best way to continue communicating with your angels is by keeping a positive mindset. When I first started communicating, I didn't think about my mindset. I felt lost, didn't have high self-esteem, and didn't feel that I was worthy enough to achieve my goals. Even though I worked hard and tried to remain dedicated to my goals, I found myself thinking negative thoughts. I would wake up in the morning and wonder what mistake I would make. I clung on to my mistakes — even the ones I had made years before — because I felt this was the only true way I'd become a better person.

I always believed in God and angels, but I never noticed their signs or even believed they tried to communicate with the living until I had a dream. I was walking down a gravel road at dawn. There were angels standing on the side of the road. I never looked in their direction, but I always saw them through the corner of my eyes as I passed. Once I reached the end of the road, I saw an ocean and a big white light coming from the sky. I looked up to the light and felt drawn to it. I couldn't take my eyes off the light, and I didn't understand what it was until I stood in front of me and waved its large wings. I woke up at that moment and heard a voice in my head say, "Trust us, for we are always with you." I wanted to push the dream out of my mind because I thought it was strange, but my heart kept telling me to believe.

A couple of days later, I was telling a friend about my dream, and she gave me a book on angels and how they communicate. I read the book and then started my own research. Soon, I was following my intuition and writing down the most common angel numbers I saw. Once I started following their messages, my mindset began to transform from negative to positive. Not only did I believe that angels communicated with me, but I also believed in myself. I became more determined to continue my studies, write, and reach any goal that I set for myself.

I continue to focus on my mindset and not just through angel meditation. I take time during the day to focus on my thoughts, write in a gratitude journal at the end of the day, eat healthy, get enough sleep, and focus on self-care.

The way I developed a positive mindset is different from your story. For instance, you might not care to write in a journal and always take time to focus on yourself. In this instance, you might want other ideas to incorporate into your life.

One tip for developing a positive mindset is to create a morning routine. Start your day by sitting up and thinking about one good task you want to do today. For example, do you want to focus on communicating with more compassion? You might decide to tell yourself you'll surprise one person with a nice gift. From your thought, develop a plan of action. After this, you can check your phone, get ready for your day, eat a healthy breakfast, and carry on with your daily schedule. But remember to check in with your good task throughout the day. Ask yourself whether you've completed it or you're following your action plan.

Another tip is to focus on positive affirmations. Many people start their day by reading a positive quote because it sets the tone for the rest of their day. But you don't have to limit this moment to your morning. You can also carry a book of affirmations with you or Google an affirmation that'll make you feel better after a negative event.

Focus on the positive in your life, no matter how small. For example, you're walking down the street and you see a penny on the sidewalk. Not only is this a sign from your angels, but it's also a positive moment in your day. It might mean that your luck is about to change, your thoughts are manifesting into reality, or your angels want you to know that you're on the right path.

Other than a positive mindset, you can also strengthen communication by remaining relaxed throughout your day. You already know the importance of relaxation during communication. The more you feel relaxed, the easier communication will become. In fact, you can find yourself talking to your guardian angel as you're driving down the road because you hear what they're saying in your head. You don't need to concentrate on meditating to hear them.

It's also a good idea to cleanse your home. All you need to do is buy a sage stick, open a couple of windows or a door, and move the smoke from the sage around your home. You don't have to say anything as you sage, but you can say something like

"I am removing all negativity from my home. Only love and light can stay." Think of cleansing your home like clearing your mind before you start meditating. You'll also notice that your home feels more positive, and it's easier to declutter your mind after a cleanse. Personally, I perform a cleanse at least once a month, more often if I feel that I notice a growing amount of negativity in my life.

One of my favorite tips for stronger communication is to create a keyword every day. When you wake up in the morning, say out loud, "Angels, today the keyword is *purple*." This will let the higher powers know that when you say "purple," you're calling them for their help.

Finally, never stop asking questions. The more questions you ask, the stronger your lines of connection will become. The higher powers love to hear from you, no matter what question you ask or what help you need from them. They are here for you.

GUIDED MEDITATION EXAMPLE

To raise your vibration with the higher powers, you need to continue guided meditations. You don't always need a request to communicate with your angels. Sometimes you can use meditation just to strengthen your connection.

> *As always, start by finding a comfortable spot. You can include candles or add some soothing and relaxing music to help your mind and body feel calmer. Candles can always help bring your mind back to reality once your meditation is over because its aroma will fill the room.*
>
> *When you want to raise your vibration with your angels, start by focusing on your breathing. You'll focus more on your breathing with this type of meditation than you did with any previous meditations. As you're breathing, you'll start to notice a light coming from the universe. It'll become brighter and brighter as you continue to focus on the rhythm of your breathing. The light may not be white. It may be purple, blue, green, or any color of the angel who is wishing to connect with you.*
>
> *The brighter the light becomes, the closer it*

is to your body. Once you start to feel the warm energy from the light, imagine it flowing throughout your body. Once it becomes a blanket over you, the angel has fulfilled the vibration and will slowly start to go back into the universe. The light will become dimmer, but the light within you will continue to shine brightly.

Once you no longer see the angel's light, it's time to bring yourself back to reality. Start by focusing on the smell of the room, the sound of the music, and the feeling of your fingers and toes. Slowly open your eyes and then continue with your day.

Now that you know the process of raising your vibrations with your angels, it's time to get started on the meditation.

Lie down and get comfortable. Keep your back straight but relaxed. Place one hand on your stomach and the other on your chest. Focus on your breathing. Breathe in, breathe out, in and then out. Find the rhythm of your breathing as you notice your hand move with your chest. Follow the movement as you slowly breathe in and out.

Breathe deeply in through your nose and slowly out your mouth. Take a few deep, slow breaths, allowing the negativity to leave your body like a dark cloud. Breathe positive, calming air through your nose and release the negative energy out your mouth with a slow breath. Continue breathing in and out, in and out until your breath looks clear.

All the negative energy is released from your body as it starts to feel soft. Your limbs are heavy as your arms slowly glide to your side. Now, focus on the rhythm of your slow breaths. Breathe in, breathe out, breathe in, breathe out.

Allow the vibrations of the room to enter your body as you start to see a bright light coming toward you. The light becomes brighter, brighter, brighter. You begin to feel the warmth of the light on your skin. Your body soaks up the warmth. It enters through your skin and into your body. It slowly flows through your veins and into your cells. It flows along with your blood.

The light becomes brighter. Your room is filled with a warm, loving, and peaceful light. The light continues to flow through your body, filling every inch with a caring and warm feeling. The light makes its way back out of your body through your fingers, toes, and head. It covers your body like a warm and loving blanket.

Let the energy fill your body, mind, and spirit as the angel completes the connection. Slowly, you see the light start to fade from your room and back into the universe. The light from the angel becomes dimmer, but your body continues its warm, loving, and peaceful glow.

Once the light of the angel is back into the universe, bring your mind back to your physical environment. Notice the aroma of the room as you start to hear the calming music. Slowly wiggle your fingers and toes as you begin to feel your body's sensations coming alive with the energy from the angel. Focus on your breathing. Notice the rhythm as you start to raise your hands slowly back up to your stomach and chest. Feel the clothing on your skin as your hands move up and down with each breath. Slowly open your eyes and thank the angel for helping you raise your vibrations. Stretch your body as you slowly sit up and continue with your day.

CONCLUSION

You might feel overwhelmed with information, but I know you also feel more confident and calm. One of the most important characteristics of the higher powers is that they hold the ability to make you feel better when you're learning about them. It's one of the main reasons why people continue to dive into this topic. The more you connect with your angels, the better you start to feel — and I'm not just talking physically.

In the introduction, I promised that you would learn how to start communicating with the higher powers, and you now have this ability. You know how angels and guardian angels communicate to you. You understand that it's a two-way street and you need to put in the effort just as they're working hard to reach you.

You now understand the difference between archangels, angels, guardian angels so you can effectively communicate with all of them. You understand that you need to call the archangels and angels to help you, but your guardian angels help you throughout your day. Of course, this doesn't mean that you don't use guided meditation to speak with them when you need clarity or want to strengthen your connection.

You know that the seven main archangels and the different types of angels all have their specific powers and duties to help keep you safe and reach your life's mission. They all work closely with your guardian angels to ensure that you have what you need and requested to the best of their abilities.

There are many important points from this book that I want you to remember, but here are a few key takeaways.

First, you have to have a clear and open mind. You need to believe what you're learning because this will help your messages come through as clearly as possible. This means you don't doubt what you're feeling, hearing, and seeing. For example, if you see a bright white light in the form of an angel in your mind's eye, believe that it's one of the higher powers visiting you. Try to connect with them. Ask them what message they have for you.

Second, never stop learning. You don't need to read countless books or do hours of research to learn about your angels. All you need to do is read as much as you feel necessary and communicate with your angels. You should also listen to your instincts. For instance, if you feel that you have three angels with you every day, then believe.

Third, you need to follow a guided meditation script that's comfortable for you. In fact, you might create your own. Personally, I used a couple of guided angel meditations, and then I started following my instincts to connect with them. Each time I meditate, I feel the lines of connection growing stronger so I continue to follow what I feel.

Fourth, don't let anyone tell you what you should believe. When I first started learning about angel communication, I let a few people that I respected tell me what to believe. Instead of taking their words and reflecting on them, I felt that they were experts so they knew it all. Connecting with the higher powers and the universe isn't like learning how to cook or become a mechanic. There are no written laws or rules that you have to attach to what you feel is right. You can simply believe something because you feel that it's right in your gut. For example, you can believe that guardian angels and spirit guides are the same because you had a dream and interpret it this way.

Finally, it's important to be patient with the higher powers. They might give you a sign after a meditation session, but this doesn't mean they will directly answer your question. It can take time for them to give you an answer for several reasons. For example, if you're asking them to help you financially, they can't directly deposit money into your bank account. You need to follow their guidance so you can build your financial wealth. It might take years because their mission is to make sure that you're promoted at the company you work for or they want you to start your own business. This all takes time, so they will consistently send you messages to let you know that they're with you, they know your dreams, and they want you to continue working hard to make your thoughts a reality.

One final note before you continue on your journey

CONCLUSION | 89

is to be proud of where you stand now. Even if you have blocks in communication, you're working to overcome them, and this is already strengthening your connection. You've taken a powerful step in opening the doorway to reaching the higher powers and feeling more attune with them and the universe. From here, you'll only feel the benefits from the universe's energies as you continue along your path and fulfill your life's mission.

REFERENCES

Bernstein, G. (2020). *10 simple and beautiful ways to connect with your spirit guides.* https://gabbybernstein.com/spirit-guides/

Demers, D. (n.d.). *The 7 archangels and their meanings.* Belief Net. https://www.beliefnet.com/inspiration/angels/galleries/the-7-archangels-and-their-meanings.aspx

Gaia. (2019). *7 things that are blocking your spirit guides.* https://www.gaia.com/article/7-things-are-blocking-your-spirit-guides

Hopler, W. (2019). *How to recognize Archangel Chamuel.* Learn Religions. https://www.learnreligions.com/how-to-recognize-archangel-chamuel-124273

Hopler, W. (2019). *How to recognize Ariel, Angel of Nature.* Learn Religions. https://www.learnreligions.com/how-to-recognize-archangel-ariel-124271

Hoy, T. (2017). *Spirit guides: 5 powerful benefits of surrounding yourself with them.* Tanahoy. https://www.tanahoy.com/benefits-of-surrounding-yourself-with-spirit-guides/

Inspiration Divination. (n.d.) How do angels communicate with us? https://www.inspirationdivination.com/how-do-angels-communicate-with-us/

Keen. (n.d.). *What is the difference between a spirit guide and an angel?* https://www.keen.com/articles/psychic/what-is-the-difference-between-spirit-guide-and-angel

Richardson, T. (2020). *How to effectively communicate with your spirit guides.* Mind Body Green. https://www.mindbodygreen.com/0-17129/how-to-effectively-communicate-with-your-spirit-guides.html

Richardson, T. (n.d.). *11 types of angels for every need.* Belief Net. https://www.beliefnet.com/inspiration/angels/galleries/11-types-of-angels-for-every-need.aspx

Richardson, T. (n.d.). *7 things you should know about guardian angels.* Belief Net. https://www.beliefnet.com/inspiration/angels/galleries/7-things-you-should-know-about-guardian-angels.aspx

Soul Gateway. (n.d.). *8 ways to connect with your spirit guides and angels.* https://soultruthgateway.com/blog/8-ways-to-connect-with-your-spirit-guides-and-angels

Tooke, A. (2016). *6 main differences between angels and spirit guides.* The Angel Mystic. https://theangelmystic.co.uk/6-main-differences-angels-spirit-guides/

Virtue, D. (2008). *8 ways to recognize Archangel Michael.* Belief Net. https://www.beliefnet.com/inspiration/angels/2008/12/8-ways-to-recognize-archangel-michael.aspx

Virtue, D. (2010). *8 signs from Archangel Raphael.* Belief Net. https://www.beliefnet.com/inspiration/angels/2010/06/healing-miracles-of-archangel-raphael.aspx

White, L. (n.d.). *5 surprising roles of guardian angels.* Belief Net. https://www.beliefnet.com/inspiration/angels/galleries/5-surprising-roles-of-guardian-angels.aspx

www.ingramcontent.com/pod-product-compliance
Lightning Source LLC
Chambersburg PA
CBHW052208090526
44583CB00016BA/1911